Wright Sites

A Guide to Frank Lloyd Wright
Public Places

D1360334

WRIGHT SITES

Edited by
Arlene Sanderson

The Frank Lloyd Wright
Building Conservancy

The Preservation Press

Cover photo courtesy of Steelcase Inc.
Veranda entrance to the Meyer May house, Grand Rapids, Michigan

Design by Bergh Jensen & Associates, Seattle

The Preservation Press
National Trust for Historic Preservation
1785 Massachusetts Avenue, N.W.
Washington, D.C. 20036

The National Trust for Historic Preservation is the only private, nonprofit organization chartered by Congress to encourage public participation in the preservation of
sites, buildings, and objects significant in American history and culture. In carrying
out this mission, the National Trust fosters an appreciation of the diverse character
and meaning of our American cultural heritage and preserves and revitalizes the
livability of our communities by leading the nation in saving America's historic
environments.

Support for the National Trust is provided by membership dues, contributions, and
a matching grant from the National Park Service, U.S. Department of the Interior,
under provisions of the National Historic Preservation Act of 1966. The opinions
expressed here do not necessarily reflect the views or policies of the Interior
Department.

Printed in 97 96 95 94 93   5 4 3

Library of Congress Cataloging-in-Publication Data
Wright sites: a guide to Frank Lloyd Wright public places/edited by Arlene
Sanderson.
        p.   cm.
    Includes index.
    ISBN 0-89133-231-6
    1. Wright, Frank Lloyd, 1867-1959—Themes, motives.
    2. Architecture—United States—Guide-books.   I. Sanderson, Arlene, 1953-
    NA737.W7W75 1991
    720'.92—dc20   91-18571
                                                        CIP

Foreword

Wright Sites: A Guide to Frank Lloyd Wright Public Places is a publication of the Frank Lloyd Wright Building Conservancy, a nationally constituted body comprised of Wright homeowners, curators, architects, preservationists, lawyers, historians and others who are committed to the preservation and restoration of Wright's extraordinary architectural legacy.

Preserving Wright's work is a formidable task. One of every seven Wright-designed buildings has been demolished and many of the 400 that survive are threatened. For the individuals and organizations who care for these treasured structures, the financial, legal and ethical complexities of their charge are often overwhelming. By forging a network of organizations and specialists who can offer professional expertise and technical assistance, the Conservancy is helping to share the burden of saving these vulnerable structures. The Conservancy is concerned with all Wright designs, but a guide to publicly accessible structures seemed essential because it is there, at the sites, that so many are won over by Wright's genius.

It is axiomatic in architectural history that great buildings must be experienced firsthand in order to be fully appreciated, and this is especially true of Wright's work. At an early age, Wright discovered that architecture could be symphonic in nature, that building parts should relate to each other, and that each part should relate to the whole.

Building "parts" to Wright were not merely walls, windows and doors, they were all of the essential considerations of architecture — structure, space, materials, the site, the furnishings, light and detailing. So closely did Wright adhere to this design philosophy that his buildings are themselves interrelated as parts of the totality that is his life's work. Thus the pinwheel configuration present in the plan of his Oak Park home of 1889 — one of his earliest buildings — is fully realized in the spiraling form of the Guggenheim Museum some 60 years later; the design of a table in the Darwin Martin house evokes the principal elevation of the building; the imprint of a concrete block from the Freeman house refers tantalizingly to the building's plan. Wright's architecture is filled with such discoveries large and small.

Widely dispersed across the continent, these sites stand as an invitation to all to know this great architect in his element — a truly American architecture.

Jack Quinan
Architectural Historian
State University of New York
at Buffalo

Preface

The study of Frank Lloyd Wright may begin with books and photographs, but the uniqueness of his contribution to American architecture can only be appreciated by stepping through the open doors of his buildings to experience the reality of the spaces.

Today one of every eight surviving structures designed by Wright, America's most renowned architect, is open to the public. The 50 sites included in this guide document the phenomenal diversity and creative genius of the man whose career spanned seven decades and resulted in more than 500 executed works. These sites include former private residences, office buildings, cultural institutions, houses of worship, and public works projects. They provide a rich and varied visual record of his evolving concept of organic architecture, beginning with his early explorations of Shingle Style and Sullivanesque forms and his distinctive Prairie designs of the early 1900s followed by the California experiments in textile block, the celebrated masterpieces of the 1930s, and the refined Usonians of his later life.

Stewardship of these properties is equally diverse. Some buildings are owned by nonprofit foundations, others by educational institutions, several by government agencies, and still others by corporations or private individuals. Many properties must rely on tourism to fund restoration and operating programs. All of the owners should be saluted for their commitment to public education about Wright. Without their dedication and the energy and leadership of community volunteers, these opportunities would not be available to us nor would this book have been possible. Their thorough study and unique insights contributed immeasurably to this publication.

We also wish to acknowledge the research of numerous Wright historians and scholars, including Jeanette Fields, David Gebhard, Henry-Russell Hitchcock, Jonathan Lipman, Grant Manson, Jack Quinan, Vincent Scully, Jr., John Sergeant, Paul Sprague, and William Allin Storrer. We are indebted as well to David Hohman for the vision that moved this project forward, to Jean Eckenfels for her editorial expertise, to John Thorpe for his critical review of portions of the text, and to Sara-Ann Briggs for technical assistance with the manuscript.

This guidebook contains nearly all of the Wright-designed buildings in the United States currently open to the public. Future editions will include newly opened properties. The dates listed reflect the design of the structure and may not coincide with the year of completion.

Guided tours or interpretive materials are available at most sites. Please phone ahead to obtain the most up-to-date information on tours so that your visit will be as pleasant and rewarding as possible.

A portion of the proceeds from this book will benefit the Frank Lloyd Wright Building Conservancy, a nonprofit organization dedicated to the preservation of all remaining Wright structures.

Judith Trent
Executive Director
Frank Lloyd Wright Building Conservancy

WRIGHT SITES

Stanley and Mildred Rosenbaum House

601 Riverview Drive Florence, Alabama 35630
(205) 764.5274

1939

Tours by appointment only • Adults $5; seniors and students $4

In his Usonian homes, Wright answered the challenge of designing a functional, affordable dwelling for the middle-class American family. Between 1936 and 1941, Wright designed 57 Usonian homes; the Rosenbaum house is one of 26 that were completed.

The exterior is primarily cypress, and the T-shaped plan includes a 20-foot, cantilevered carport. This residence differs from earlier Usonian designs in the total absence of a basement and greater spaciousness of the interior. Features include recessed lighting, decorative fretwork, and built-in cabinetry and furnishings. Wright designed a major addition for the home in 1948.

This private residence has been renovated and is listed on the National Register of Historic Places.

Arizona Biltmore Hotel and Cottages

24th Street and Missouri Phoenix, Arizona 85016
(602) 954.2504
Guided tours in conjunction with Gold Room Buffet Luncheon:
November through April, Monday, Wednesday, and Friday at 1:30 p.m.
Reservations required • Tours at other times by appointment only
• Buffet Luncheon tour $13.95 per person. $25 per tour for groups of
fewer than 25; $50 per tour for groups of 26 or more • Handicapped
accessible

1927

The Arizona Biltmore is generally recognized as a collaborative effort between Wright and Albert Chase McArthur, a former draftsman in Wright's Oak Park studio. McArthur's signature appears on drawings for the project, and he was responsible for the plan of the hotel.

McArthur called on Wright for technical assistance with the design and engineering of the buildings' concrete block system. Wright had experimented with the use of cast concrete blocks joined with metal rods in the design of several Los Angeles houses. The Biltmore gave him his only opportunity to demonstrate the possibilities of the system on a large scale.

When the stock market crashed, the hotel was sold to the Wrigley chewing gum family. In 1973, the building was sold again, just before a construction-related fire destroyed the entire fourth floor and copper roof. Taliesin Associated Architects supervised the reconstruction and restoration. Original drawings were used to reproduce the interiors.

The 500-room luxury resort, with three pools, golf courses and a conference center, is managed by Westin Hotels and Resorts.

::

First Christian Church

6750 North Seventh Avenue Phoenix, Arizona 85013
(602) 246.9206
Tours by appointment only • Free • Handicapped accessible

1950

Wright's design for the First Christian Church reflects his belief that the modern church should be a building without historical or sectarian reference.

The triangle, symbolizing the Christian Trinity, is essential to the conceptual and physical design of this structure. Twenty-three triangular, steel and concrete pillars support the building. The pyramidal roof and spire rise 77 feet above a second, but narrower range of triangular columns that frame clerestory windows. Light filters through the spire's colored glass insets onto the floor of the diamond-shaped sanctuary.

Wright designed the 120-foot, freestanding bell tower with four unequal sides, giving the structure a triangular appearance.

Completed in 1972, 13 years after Wright's death, the church was part of an earlier commission for a university for Southwest Christian Seminary. The church is the only part of the original plan to be built.

::

Taliesin West

4 ARIZONA

Cactus Road and 108th Street Scottsdale, Arizona 85261
(602) 860.2700
Guided, one-hour tours: October through May, Monday through
Thursday, 1 to 4 p.m., hourly; Friday through Sunday, 9 a.m. to 4 p.m.,
hourly—$10 per person. June through September, daily, 8 to 11 a.m.,
hourly—$6 per person • Guided half-day, in-depth tours by reservation
only. Limited to 20 people per tour. Call for information

1937

In 1937, Wright purchased 600 acres of rugged land in the Sonoran Desert at the foot
of the McDowell Mountains. He established a kind of experimental desert camp that
would serve as his winter home until his death in 1959.

Over the years, the quarter-mile complex was continually altered and
expanded to comprise living quarters, studios, workshops, offices, apartments,
theaters, gardens, terraces and independent residences. Constructed of stone,
cement, redwood and canvas, the buildings grew out of the desert terrain. Their
angled roofs, exposed beams and rubble walls mirrored the colors, textures and
forms of the surrounding landscape. As the buildings took on greater permanence,
steel and plaster replaced the less durable materials.

A National Historic Landmark, Taliesin West, like Taliesin East, is owned and
operated by the Frank Lloyd Wright Foundation, along with an architectural school
and archives. Taliesin Associated Architects is the professional firm associated with
the Foundation.

Grady Gammage Memorial Auditorium

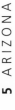

Arizona State University Apache Boulevard at Mill Avenue
Tempe, Arizona 85287-0105
(602) 965.5062
Guided tours Monday through Saturday,1:30 to 3:30 p.m. • Free
• Handicapped accessible • Gift store

1959

During the last year of his life, Wright received the only commission he was to earn from the state in which he lived. This last public space is a circular, 3000-seat center for the performing arts with a concert hall, proscenium theater, classrooms and offices.

Two, 200-foot pedestrian bridges rise from the adjacent lawn and sunken parking area to the circular building. Inside, the vast stage accommodates a full symphony orchestra, chorus and pipe organ. Seating in the auditorium is divided between the main floor, grand tier and balcony. A 145-foot girder supports the upper-level seating, which is detached from the rear wall, allowing sound to encircle the audience.

The building, named for a former president of the university, was completed in 1959 at a total cost of nearly $5 million.

Anderton Court Shops

CALIFORNIA

6

332 North Rodeo Drive Beverly Hills, California 90210
No organized tour program • Shops open Monday through Saturday,
10 a.m. to 6 p.m.

1952

In the 1940s, Wright began to develop a scheme for the Guggenheim Museum based on a hexagonal ramp system. This concept was modified for use on a smaller scale at the Anderton Court Shops.

The ramp, which encircles a light well, provides access to shops on four levels. The ramp's solid exterior wall visually links the angled glass sections of the building's facade. A stylized pylon rises through the light well and extends well beyond the rooftop.

The upper level canopy and signage are later additions not of Wright's design.

Aline Barnsdall House *Hollyhock House*

4808 Hollywood Boulevard Los Angeles, California 90027
(213) 662.7272
Guided tours: Tuesday, Wednesday, and Thursday, 10 and 11 a.m., noon and 1 p.m.; Saturday and Sunday, noon, 1, 2 and 3 p.m.
• Groups of 15 or more by appointment only. Foreign language tours by special arrangement • Adults $1.50; seniors $1; under 12 free when accompanied by an adult

1917

Oil heiress and theater producer Aline Barnsdall commissioned Wright to build a complex of residences, theaters, shops and apartments to serve a Los Angeles community of avant-garde artists. Barnsdall first met Wright in Chicago, where she had considered building an earlier theater. Her plans changed, however, and she purchased a 36-acre hilltop site in East Hollywood.

Hollyhock house, Barnsdall's private residence, and two guest residences were the only buildings completed of Wright's vast and elaborate plan. The house was built of hollow tile, stucco and wood. Hollyhocks, Barnsdall's favorite flower, inspired the stylized, cast concrete ornamental bands on the exterior walls, as well as the capitals on the courtyard piers and the finials projecting from the roof.

The T-shaped main block of the house comprises an entry loggia and living room, which is flanked by a library and music room. Two opposing wings, which extend from the main living area, contain the bedrooms, dining room and service areas of the home. These spaces open onto a large courtyard garden that terminates in a circular pool. The long, low walls of the terraces and patio anchor the building to the site and recall Wright's earlier Prairie style residences in the Midwest.

In 1927, Barnsdall donated Hollyhock house, one of the guest residences and 11 acres of what is now Barnsdall Art Park to the City of Los Angeles.

Ennis-Brown House

2655 Glendower Avenue Los Angeles, California 90027-1114
(213) 660.0607
Guided tours by appointment: second Saturday of January, March, May,
July, September and November, 11:45 a.m. to 3:45 p.m. • Special tours
by appointment only • Adults $10; seniors, students, and children $5;
children in arms free

1923

Wright had been experimenting with the potential of precast concrete block for
more than a decade when in the 1920s, he adopted the material for the design of
several California projects. The medium was well suited to the creation of buildings
in a regional style that reflected the cultural history of the West and could be
fabricated from local materials.

The house Charles and Mabel Ennis commissioned in 1923 for a half-acre
site in the Hollywood Hills is the largest of the Los Angeles concrete block dwellings.
Constructed of 16-inch square blocks, joined with metal reinforcing rods, the building
rises in stages from an enormous platform buttressed by a retaining wall. The
division of the facade in zones of smooth and patterned blocks continues on the
interior walls.

A low, dark entry leads to the upper level, where the loggia, living
room and dining room are joined in a continuous space that Wright called
"the great room."

In 1980, the owner, A. Oliver Brown, donated the house to the Trust for
Preservation of Cultural Heritage, which is responsible for the building's
restoration.

Samuel Freeman House

1962 Glencoe Way Los Angeles, California 90068
(213) 851.0671
Guided tours for groups only, by appointment and as restoration
permits • Five person minimum, $10 per person

1924

Sam and Harriet Freeman were newlywed members of Los Angeles' artistic avant-garde when they first encountered Wright's architecture at Hollyhock house, the home of theater producer Aline Barnsdall.

When the Freemans asked Wright to design their own house, he used his new textile-block construction system. The experiment went considerably over time and budget with the result that the Freemans turned to the Austrian architect and former Wright apprentice, Rudolph Schindler, for the extensive furnishings and various remodelings.

The design of the house takes advantage of the steep and narrow lot. The building appears to be a single story from the street, but is actually constructed on two levels. The space of the main living area extends outward onto a balcony and the lower level bedrooms open onto a terrace. Large areas of glass also serve to visually expand the modest-sized interior.

The walls are constructed of some 11,000 concrete blocks, cast on site and joined with metal reinforcing rods. The combination of solid and perforated blocks creates constantly changing patterns of light and shadow within the house.

Harriet Freeman willed the house to the University of Southern California's School of Architecture. The school is responsible for the building's restoration and maintenance.

V.C. Morris Gift Shop

10 CALIFORNIA

Circle Gallery (currently)
140 Maiden Lane San Francisco, California 94108
(415) 989.2100
No organized tours • Open to visitors during business hours: Monday through Saturday,10 a.m. to 6 p.m.; Sunday, noon to 5 p.m.• Groups of 10 or more by appointment only • Handicapped accessible • No photographs

1948

The design of the Guggenheim Museum, commissioned in 1943, was far from complete when California businessman V.C. Morris previewed the radical plan and asked Wright to adapt the concept for a San Francisco gift shop.   The imposing exterior wall of tightly knit Roman brick with its monumental masonry arch contrasts dramatically with the expansive, light-filled interior. A circular ramp leads to the upper level and provides additional display area along its length.

A retail space until 1983, the building now houses a gallery of contemporary art.

Marin County Civic Center

North San Pedro Road at U.S. 101 San Rafael, California 94903
(415) 499.7407
Self-guided tours during regular business hours, Monday through
Friday, 9 a.m. to 5 p.m. • Guided and group tours by appointment
only • Handicapped accessible

1957

The Marin County Board of Supervisors purchased 140 acres north of San Rafael
intending to centralize 13 widely dispersed county departments under one roof. They
commissioned Wright to develop a master plan for the site. In 1957, he presented a
design for the Administration Building and the Hall of Justice, as well as preliminary
plans for a theater, auditorium, fairgrounds and lagoon.

Construction had just begun at the time of his death in 1959. William Wesley
Peters and Aaron Green, a San Francisco architect, became project directors.

Wright's plan specified a 584-foot Administration Building and an 880-foot
Hall of Justice that would bridge the valleys between three adjacent hills. The focal
point and center of the plan was a flattened dome, 80 feet in diameter, crowned by
a 172-foot gold tower containing a smokestack and communications antennae.

The Administration Building houses government offices as well as a library
and the California History Room.   The Hall of Justice, completed in 1969, contains
courtrooms, government offices and the county jail.

The buildings were constructed of precast, prestressed concrete and steel at
a cost of $16.7 million. The exterior screen walls are divided into rhythmic arcades
and circular openings. The circular motif is continued in the grillework and gold
spheres rimming the roof edge. Later construction includes a post office, the Veterans
Memorial Auditorium, an exhibition building and a maintenance facility.

::

Florida Southern College

111 Lake Hollingsworth Drive Lakeland, Florida 33801-5698
(813) 680.4116
Self-guided walking tour with map available at Watson Administration
Building, free • Guided group tours by appointment only, $5 per person
• Handicapped accessible

1938

On land once occupied by an orange grove, Wright set out to design a "truly American campus." In 1938, Dr. Ludd Spivey, president of Florida Southern College, commissioned Wright to produce a master plan for the 80-acre, lakeside campus of this small, Methodist school.

Over the next 20 years, buildings of Wright's design took form, beginning in 1940 with the Anne Pfeiffer Chapel, which is both the tallest building of the complex and the focal point of the plan. The chapel's angular, vertical silhouette provides a strong visual counterpoint to the low, flat-roofed seminar building of 1941 and the circular reading room of the Roux Library that followed in 1945.

Other Wright-designed buildings are the Watson Administration Building, the Ordway Building with its amphitheater, the small Danforth Chapel, and the Polk County Science Building, which contains the only planetarium of Wright's design.

The buildings are uniformly constructed of tan-colored, reinforced concrete. The contrast between smooth, textured and perforated block, and the use of colored glass insets are important components of Wright's design.

Covered esplanades link this exceptionally large collection of Wright-designed buildings. The light wells and large planters of these flat-roofed walkways create a garden-like setting appropriate to the site.

::

W.A. Pettit Memorial Chapel

North Main at Harrison Belvidere, Illinois 61008
(815) 547.7642
No organized tours • Cemetery hours Monday through Friday, 8 a.m.
to noon and 1 to 4 p.m. • Groups of 10 or more by appointment only

1906

Emma Glasner Pettit commissioned Wright to design a chapel for the Belvidere
Cemetery, 80 miles northwest of Chicago, as a memorial to her husband Dr.
William A. Pettit. The small, chaste Prairie style building served as a gathering
place for services in the early 1900s when funeral homes were not widely
available. A projecting porch offered shelter for visitors during inclement
weather as well.

The building's architectural features include a cruciform plan, horizontal
wood trim on the exterior and interior surfaces, a large, central brick fireplace,
and art glass windows.

The chapel was restored in 1981.

James Charnley House

Skidmore, Owings & Merrill Foundation
1365 North Astor Street Chicago, Illinois 60610
(312) 951.8006
Self-guided tours by appointment, Monday through Friday, 9 a.m.
to 5 p.m.• Free

1891

Frank Lloyd Wright was the chief draftsman in the offices of Dankmar Adler and Loui
Sullivan when James Charnley commissioned the design of this house. The firm
specialized in large commercial buildings, and smaller residential commissions were
often assigned to Wright. Sullivan, a personal friend of the Charnleys, probably
reviewed Wright's drawings, and the house is the product of their collaboration.
        In the design of this building, Wright said he first recognized the decorative
value of the plain surface. The uncompromising simplicity of the building's exterior
no doubt stood in stark contrast to the neighboring facades on this prestigious
Chicago street.
        The interior plan is equally straightforward. A dramatic, open stair-hall rise
three floors to a central skylight. The first floor space is evenly divided with the livin
room to the north and the dining room to the south. Bedrooms were located on the
second floor, servants quarters on the third and the kitchen in the basement.
The decorative ornament on the wood trim is Sullivanesque.
        The house has been painstakingly restored by Skidmore,
Owings and Merrill.
::

Frederick C. Robie House

5757 S. Woodlawn Chicago, Illinois 60637
(312) 702.8374
Guided tours daily at noon • Groups of 10 or more by appointment only
• Adults $3; seniors and students $1; children under 10 free

1908

Robie was a pragmatic businessman who wanted a fireproof, affordable, functional home. Wright responded with a radical plan that both satisfied his client and fully integrated the design elements developed in his earlier Prairie School residences.

The dominant horizontal axis of the building complements the site, a long, narrow city lot. The building rises in three planes from a concrete watertable. The dense Roman brick masonry was softened by the foliage that trailed from the planters and urns designed as part of the exterior walls.

The first floor contained a playroom, billiard room and attached garage. The main living area was located on the second floor. The long open expanse of space on this level is interrupted only by the fireplace block separating the dining and living room areas. Bedrooms were on the smaller third floor. At each level, doors and windows opened onto terraces, balconies or porches, extending the living space out into nature.

Wright designed the house in its entirety, complete with furnishings, light fixtures, rugs and art glass. This National Historic Landmark, which is owned by the University of Chicago, remains among the most celebrated of Wright's Prairie style designs.

LaSalle and Adams Streets Chicago, Illinois 60604
No organized tour program • Building hours Monday through
Friday, 8 a.m. to 6 p.m. • Handicapped accessible

1905

Wright had more than a casual acquaintance with the 10-story office building
designed by Chicago architects Burnham and Root in the late 1880s. He had
maintained an office here from 1898-99, as did his clients William Winslow and the
Luxfer Prism Company. Edward C. Waller, another client, managed the building, and
he commissioned Wright to remodel the entrance.

Wright replaced the intricate cast-iron ornament of the original lobby,
facing the interior surfaces with marble. The curvilinear patterns of the incised
and gilded surface decoration reflect Wright's early training with Sullivan and
complement designs found elsewhere in the building. The large, geometric urns and
suspended light fixtures were also designed and installed during remodeling.
The building has undergone extensive restoration.

::

Frank L. Smith Bank

First National Bank of Dwight (currently)
122 West Street Dwight, Illinois 60420
(815) 584.1212
No organized tours • Open during business hours, Monday through Friday

1905

The simple dignity and solidity of this cut stone facade is consistent with Wright's belief that banks should express their own character rather than "put on the airs of a temple of worship."

The plan of this one-story, square building is straightforward and entirely functional with a central entrance, a single, large public space for transacting business, and three offices at the rear. The walls are trimmed with narrow wood strips in a spare geometric pattern. Originally a large skylight provided natural light and ventilation.

The building has been renovated by the present owners, who have recaptured some of the original design lost in earlier remodelings. They plan an addition consistent with the existing structure.

::

George Fabyan Villa

1511 Batavia Avenue Geneva, Illinois 60134
(708) 232.4811
Guided tours May 1 through October 15, Saturday, Sunday and
holidays, 1 to 5 p.m. • Weekday group tours by appointment only
• Donation welcome

1907

Wright's typical Prairie period work contrasts with his response to the constraints of
this commission from wealthy cotton-trader George Fabyan and his wife, Nelle, for
their 245-acre Fox River estate. Incorporated into the north and west sections of the
building is an earlier, L-shaped structure, which probably dictated the clapboard
siding and gable roof. The shape of the roof is reflected in the second-story windows and the decorative motif on the columns at ground level.

    The elongated, cruciform plan of the two-story, 3800-square-foot house was
more obvious before the removal of matching north and south verandas, as well as
an east veranda that afforded a grand river vista. These structures with their cement
piers and the screen fence off the south entrance visually balanced the massive,
heavily banded stucco eaves.

    A first-floor bedroom, bath and pantry are historically noteworthy. The
remaining public area is devoted to a natural history museum. A Japanese garden
and Dutch windmill elsewhere on the estate offer more evidence of the Fabyans'
varied interests.

    Since 1939 the Fabyan Estate has been owned and managed by the Kane
County Forest Preserve District, which is cooperating with the Friends of Fabyan,
a volunteer group, in the preservation and restoration of the property.

::

Ravine Bluffs Bridge

C.1915

Sylvan Road west of Franklin Road
Glencoe, Illinois 60022

The Wright-designed bridge in this North Shore suburb of Chicago originally was planned to lead to the home of Sherman Booth Sr. at 265 Sylvan Road. The home, however, was subsequently located farther north.

Booth, who was Wright's attorney, commissioned "Ravine Bluffs," a subdivision of Wright-designed homes. Only six of the residences, including Booth's, and the bridge were completed by 1921 when Booth's financial losses in the gold market brought an abrupt end to the venture.

The reinforced concrete deck of this three-span bridge accommodates a one-lane road and a pedestrian walkway with a semicircular seating area. Wright designed the low square urns and light pillars at each end.

Serious structural deterioration forced the closing of the bridge in 1977. A citizens' campaign to save the bridge from demolition was rewarded in 1985, when the bridge re-opened after a $393,000 restoration.

Wright also designed the light pillars and planters that were constructed as entrance markers to the subdivision.

::

Francisco Terrace Apartments
Archway Reconstruction

Lou Suriano

1895

Euclid Place and Lake Street
Oak Park, Illinois 60302

A semicircular arch marked the entrance to the courtyard apartments of Francisco Terrace. Commissioned by Edward Waller, the 44-unit complex provided low-cost housing for residents of Chicago's near west side.

The terra cotta ornament within the spandrels clearly reflects Wright's training with Louis Sullivan. The decorative effect is tightly framed by contrasting brickwork.

After years of neglect, Francisco Terrace was demolished in 1974. Only the arch was preserved and reconstructed at the courtyard entrance of this smaller Oak Park building.

::

Horse Show Fountain

1909

Scoville Park Fountain (currently)
Lake Street and Oak Park Avenue Oak Park, Illinois 60302

Wright's role in the design of the Horse Show Fountain is the subject of speculation. Richard Bock, the artist responsible for the sculptural ornament on a number of Wright-designed buildings of this period, is the designer of record. Bock credited Wright with suggesting the central opening to accommodate a drinking fountain. Historians generally agree that the naturalistic style of sculptural relief belongs to Bock while the overall geometric mass and proportions suggest a close collaboration between the sculptor and architect.

The present fountain is a reproduction that stands 100 feet from its original curbside location and marks the southeast boundary of Scoville Park.

Unity Temple

Melissa Ann Pinney

875 Lake Street Oak Park, Illinois 60302
(708) 848.6225
Self-guided tours Monday through Friday, 2 to 4 p.m. • Adults $3;
seniors and students $2 • Guided tours Saturday and Sunday at 2 p.m.
• Adults $5; seniors and students $3

1905

When the Unitarian Church of Oak Park burned in 1905, Wright was selected to design a new building for the congregation. He was faced with a modest budget of $45,000, a small, noisy site and the need for two buildings, one for worship and the other for socializing.

Wright's choice of reinforced concrete as a building material and the bold simplicity of the cubistic design were unprecedented. The material produced a monumental facade affording privacy and muffling street noise.

Wright's answer to the congregation's need for two buildings was straight-forward; two large spaces, a square sanctuary on the north, a rectangular meeting house on the south with access from a shared central entrance. Three different interior color schemes delineate the spaces.

The sanctuary, entered through low cloisters, was called a "jewel box" by Wright. The patterns of wood trim and art glass form a dramatic geometric composition. The space is intimate; yet the room holds 400 people with no one more than 45 feet from the pulpit.

Designated a National Historic Landmark in 1971, the building continues in use as a Unitarian Universalist Church with an active congregation.

Frank Lloyd Wright Home & Studio

23 ILLINOIS

951 Chicago Avenue Oak Park, Illinois 60302
(708) 848.1500
Guided, one-hour tours: Monday through Friday, 11 a.m., 1 and 3 p.m.;
Saturday and Sunday, 11 a.m. to 4 p.m., continuously • Adults $6;
seniors and youths 10-18 $4; children under 10 free • Groups of 10 or
more by appointment only. Call (708) 848.1978 • Other tours include a
walking tour of the Frank Lloyd Wright Prairie School Historic District
and Wright Plus, a day-long tour of 10 buildings on the third Saturday
each May ($30). Call for more information • Limited handicapped access

1889 / 1898
• No interior photography • Bookshop

Wright was a 22-year-old draftsman in the office of Chicago architect Louis Sullivan
when he borrowed $5000 from his employer to buy a corner lot and build a home for
his bride Catherine Tobin. The exterior of the house reflects an interest in the
Shingle style designs then popular on the East Coast. The building also exhibits
features that would prove essential to Wright's own philosophy of architecture; the
emphasis on geometric forms, the broad, sheltering roof, the use of natural materials
and the unity of building and site.

In 1895, Wright expanded the living space of the home by adding a dining
room and a barrel-vaulted playroom. In 1898, he joined his professional and personal
lives under one roof with the addition of a four-room studio on Chicago Avenue.

The home and studio served as a laboratory for Wright's ceaseless
experimentation with light, space, and decorative forms. In his two-story, octagonal
drafting room, Wright worked with 14 apprentices to forge a distinctly American
style of design, the Prairie School.

The home and studio complex, a National Historic Landmark, has been
restored to its 1911 design, the last year of Wright's residence in Oak Park.

Waller Gates

Lou Suriano

1901

Auvergne Place at Lake Street
River Forest, Illinois 60305

Six, rock-face, cut limestone pylons with dressed stone caps and two metal fence sections remain from the impressive entrance gate Wright designed for Edward C. Waller. A wealthy businessman and one of Wright's earliest patrons, Waller owned a six-acre estate along the Des Plaines River. In 1889, he commissioned Wright to remodel the dining room of his 24-room mansion and to design a gardener's cottage and stable.

The gates were constructed after Waller sold a portion of his land to William Winslow. Wright designed a residence for Winslow at 515 Auvergne Place in 1893. The fence sections were almost certainly fabricated from rolled steel at William Winslow's ornamental ironworks. The original construction included a double drive gate over the roadway and two flanking walk gates. Square gaslight lanterns with brass frames topped the center piers.

The gates have been partially restored. The lanterns and gates will be reproduced when funds are available.

Susan Lawrence Dana House

25 ILLINOIS

Dana-Thomas House (currently)
301 E. Lawrence Avenue Springfield, Illinois 62703
(217) 782.6776
Guided, hour-long tours daily, 9 a.m. to 4 p.m. Visitors may call day of visit to reserve a specific tour time • Groups of 10 or more by appointment only • Free • Limited handicapped access. Others may find numerous changes of level restrictive

1902-04

Heiress and activist Susan Lawrence Dana commissioned Wright to design a home suited to her prominent social position and lavish style of entertaining. She offered an unlimited budget but insisted that Wright incorporate the existing Lawrence family home into his design.

Wright responded with a 12,000-square-foot residence constructed on several levels with a double-cross axis plan. The brick exterior walls extend to the upper level where a frieze of plaster panels frames the casement windows.

The first floor, which is raised above the street, contains the main living area. The ceiling heights of the reception hall, dining room and gallery extend the full two stories of the house.

Unfettered by financial considerations, Wright achieved an unprecedented unity of interior and exterior design. He collaborated with a number of skilled artisans to produce 450 pieces of art glass and more than 100 pieces of oak furniture, as well as sculptures and frescoes.

After Dana's death, the building was purchased by the Thomas Publishing firm, and in 1981 became an official state property. Recently restored, the Dana-Thomas house is the largest and most complete of Wright's Prairie houses. The building is a National Historic Landmark.

::

Lowell Walter House *Cedar Rock*

P.O. Box One Quasqueton, Iowa 52326
(319) 934-3572
Guided tours: May 1 through October 31, Tuesday through Sunday,
11 a.m. to 5 p.m. • Groups of 15 or more by appointment only • Free
• Candlelight walk on the second Saturday each June

1945

A limestone bluff high above a bend in Iowa's Wapsipinicon River provided a dramatic setting for a complex of buildings designed for Des Moines businessman Lowell Walter and his wife Agnes.

The 11-acre site includes the main house, a two-story boat house, outdoor hearth, and entrance gate. Walter commissioned the design in 1942, but war-time restrictions delayed construction until 1948. The one-story main house, constructed of brick, glass, and walnut, is designed according to a grid; the basic unit is a five-foot-three-inch square. The roof and floor slab are concrete.

A 900-square-foot garden room served as a combined living and dining room for the Walters. Walls of glass on three sides offer a spectacular view of the river and valley floor below. Clerestory windows and skylights provide natural light and ventilation elsewhere in the house.

According to provisions in Walter's will, upon his death in 1981, Cedar Rock became the property of the Iowa Department of Natural Resources and the people of Iowa.

Henry J. Allen House

Allen-Lambe House Museum and Study Center (currently)
255 N. Roosevelt Wichita, Kansas 67208
(316) 687.1027
Guided tours by appointment only • Fee to be determined • Limited
handicapped access • No photographs

1916

Elsie Allen, wife of Kansas governor, statesman and publisher Henry J. Allen, was responsible for hiring Frank Lloyd Wright as the architect for their home. The design process probably began in 1915 at the same time Wright was at work on the Imperial Hotel in Japan. The house was completed by 1919.

The Allen residence is a late Prairie style structure. Its horizontal lines, expansive roof and massive masonry chimney recall Wright's Midwestern houses of the early 1900s. The L-shaped plan in which the main living areas open out onto a garden and the foyer with its built-in banquette and bookcase prefigure design elements found in later Usonian houses.

The one-story living room wing stands at a right angle to a longer, two-story wing that contained the first-floor dining room, kitchen, servant quarters and garage. A library, sitting rooms and bedrooms were on the second floor.

Exterior and interior walls are honey-colored brick. The use of gold leaf in the mortar joints, the predominance of windows and glass doors over walls, and the use of sweet gum wood throughout are notable interior features. The enclosed courtyard garden, lily pool and garden house are Japanese in inspiration.

The house will open to the public when restoration is complete with furnishings designed by Wright and George M. Niedecken and works of art of the period on display.

Juvenile Cultural Study Center

Harry F. Corbin Education Center (currently)
Wichita State University 21st Street Wichita, Kansas 67208
(316) 689.3737
No organized tour program • When the university is in session, the
center is open Monday through Friday, 9 a.m. to 10 p.m.; Saturday,
9 a.m. until noon

1958

Wright was commissioned in 1957 to build classroom and office space for the
university's college of education. The following year, plans were completed, but
inadequate funding delayed construction until 1963, four years after Wright's death.
     The concrete, brick and steel structure is supported by 200 pylons sunk into
a bed of unstable clay. An esplanade with a fountain and reflecting pool separates
the center's two wings. The north wing provides offices for 19 faculty members
along with conference rooms, lounges and libraries. The south wing contains seven
classrooms of varied size. Each wing has a roofed courtyard with an open skylight
through which a slender light tower extends 60 feet into the air.

::

Meyer May House

450 Madison Southeast Grand Rapids, Michigan 49503
(616) 246.4821
Guided tours: Tuesday and Thursday, 10 a.m. to 2 p.m.; Sunday,
1 to 5 p.m. • Reservations required for groups of 10 or more • Free
• Limited handicapped access

1908

Wright designed this brick residence as a family home for Meyer May, a successful Grand Rapids clothier. He sited the house close to the north lot line providing optimum light through the art glass windows and doors on the building's southern facade and maximum lawn area.

The strong horizontal lines, concrete watertable, raked mortar joints, broad overhangs and window groupings are all hallmarks of Wright's mature Prairie style houses.

Impeccably restored by the Steelcase Corporation in 1987, the home offers a unique opportunity to see an intact Prairie style house, complete with art glass, furnishings, light fixtures and carpets. The house includes a hollyhock mural by Wright collaborator and interior designer George Niedecken and two striking fireplaces with gold glass set into the mortar joints.

The building earned an American Institute of Architects' Honor Award for Restoration in 1989.

Lindholm Service Station

Best Service Station (currently)
Route 33 and Cloquet Avenue Cloquet, Minnesota 55720
(218) 879.0202
No organized tours • Open during regular business hours, 7 a.m.
to 6 p.m. daily

1956

Wright first began working on a design for a standard prefabricated gas station in the 1920s. The Lindholm Station is a variation of that prototype. The architect hoped to eliminate the frequent "eyesores" lining American highways and to develop a facility that would offer a variety of customer services in addition to selling fuel.

When opened in 1954, the station attracted notice far beyond this small northern Minnesota town, and pump sales set a new record for Phillips 66. Unique features of the steel and concrete building included the 60-foot illuminated rooftop pylon, glass observation lounge and 32-foot cantilevered copper canopy. Wright designed the canopy to hold overhead hoses, thus eliminating the need for pump islands. The plan failed because local fire codes require underground fuel storage.

The building continues to be viewed as an eccentric novelty and remains the only Wright-designed station ever completed.

::

Community Christian Church

4601 Main Street Kansas City, Missouri 64112
(816) 561.6531
Guided tours by appointment only: Monday through Friday, 9 a.m.
to 4:30 p.m. Visitors at other times must check with office • Free
• Handicapped accessible

1940

The building Wright planned for the congregation of Dr. Burris A. Jenkins was to be "the church of the future." Financial considerations, war-time shortages of materials and code restrictions greatly compromised Wright's original design. Although the architect lamented that the building was his only in shape, the structure remains highly original and continues to satisfy the needs of the congregation.

Both the exterior outline and interior space of the building are irregular. Wright developed the design from a basic parallelogram unit called a "hex." The walls are constructed of gunnite, an inexpensive, strong, fireproof and lightweight concrete. The use of this material allowed Wright to reduce the thickness of the wall to 2 3/4 inches. When joined at wide angles the walls thus have the appearance of folded planes. The original construction contained no square corners among the wall junctures. All stairwells, offices and classrooms are hexagonal.

The sanctuary's acoustical quality and seating capacity for nearly 900 people make it an attractive space for musical performances. The chapel and fellowship hall are later additions.

::

Lockridge Medical Clinic

Brown and Blade Optometrists (currently)
341 Central Avenue Whitefish, Montana 59937
No organized tour program • Building is open during regular business hours, Monday through Friday, 9 a.m. to 5 p.m.; Saturday, 9 a.m. to noon

1958

Wright's design of a one-story, brick and cast concrete medical clinic for the general practice of Drs. Lockridge, McIntyre and Whalen, has been significantly altered by subsequent owners. Shortly after the clinic was completed, Lockridge died; and in 1964 the building was converted to a bank. In 1980, the bank moved to larger quarters, and the building was divided into three professional offices.

Wright's plan provided for a central waiting room and reception area with examination and procedure rooms to the side and rear. The floor-to-ceiling glass windows of the west facade and large fireplace have been retained despite considerable changes elsewhere.

Wright's design included a white, plastic sphere that was centered between the windows at the front of the building. This sphere was half on the exterior and half on the interior like the circular brick planter supporting it. The sphere was removed, along with the interior planter, to provide space for a front walk and entrance to the bank lobby.

The square planter on the roof now houses an air conditioning unit.
The carport to the south of the building is a later addition.
::

Isadore J. and Lucille Zimmerman House

Currier Gallery of Art
192 Orange Street Manchester, New Hampshire 03104
(603) 669.6144 general information; (603) 626.4158 reservations
Guided, one-hour tours by reservation only: Thursday through Saturday,
10:30 a.m. to 2:30 p.m.; Sunday, 2 to 3:30 p.m. No children under
seven • *All tours depart the Currier Gallery* • Adults $5; seniors and
students $3; members free • Groups and disabled visitors by reservation
with three weeks notice, call (603) 669.6144 • No interior photography
• Gift shop

1950

The Zimmermans commissioned Wright to design a modest-sized home for them.
The resulting building combines features of Wright's early Prairie style houses, as
well as his Usonian designs.

The low, horizontal roof gives the house an appearance of exceptional
length, although it has only 1775 square feet of living space. The brick, cast
concrete and cypress dwelling is sited diagonally on a one-acre lot. A high,
continuous band of windows set in a contrasting color, concrete block distinguishes
the street facade while preserving the privacy of those inside. The extensive use of
glass on the garden facade, in comparison, opens the interior to the outside world.

Wright also designed all the freestanding and built-in furniture, the textiles
and gardens. The built-in furnishings, mitered corner windows and dramatic
changes in ceiling height make this small house seem larger.

The building was bequeathed to the Currier Gallery of Art by the
Zimmermans and has been partially restored.

::

Darwin D. Martin House

125 Jewett Parkway Buffalo, New York 14214
(716) 831.2406
Regular tour schedule temporarily suspended. Please call for information

1904

The Martin house like the Dana house completed the same year, was a grand and ambitious design to satisfy a wealthy and socially prominent client. Martin, however, proved not only a sympathetic patron, but also a friend who would support and sustain Wright through great personal turmoil.

Martin's private residence was part of a larger complex of six buildings Wright designed for this large lot on Jewett Parkway. The greenhouse, conservatory, garage and pergola were demolished in 1960. A smaller residence designed for Martin's sister remains nearby.

The main horizontal axis of the monumental Roman brick house parallels the parkway. The vertical dimension of the building is compressed by the low hip roof and exceptionally broad eaves. The living room, dining room, and library are to the right of the entrance hall; a second living room, office and kitchen are to the left. Bedrooms are located on the second floor, and the basement served as a ballroom.

The coordinated effect of the Wright-designed art glass windows, furnishings, light fixtures and rugs was spectacular. The lavish mosaic surround of the main fireplace was executed by Orlando Giannini, a Chicago artisan.

A National Historic Landmark, the Martin house is owned by the State University of New York. Restoration plans are pending.

Solomon R. Guggenheim Museum

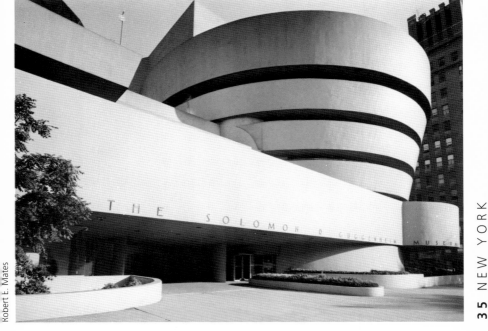

1071 Fifth Avenue New York, New York 10128
(212) 360.3500
Museum currently closed for restoration and expansion. Due to re-open in spring 1992. Museum hours will be: Daily 10 a.m. to 8 p.m.; closed Thursdays • Fee to be determined • Group and foreign language tours by appointment only • Handicapped accessible • Bookshop • Restaurant

1956

The design of few buildings has inspired the level of controversy generated by the Guggenheim Museum. Solomon R. Guggenheim commissioned the museum in 1943, but 13 years passed before ground was broken. The design and construction of the museum required some 700 sketches and an additional six sets of working drawings. Wright waged exhaustive battles with New York City officials whose outdated building codes had no relevance to his design. Finally in 1958, construction began. The museum opened shortly after Wright's death in 1959.

A gradually opening spiral, the cast concrete form was labeled a "ziggurat" by Wright. The effect is sculptural; there are no surface embellishments. The curving, streamlined exterior establishes a pattern of wall and void, corresponding to changes in level on the interior.

Inside, a quarter-mile-long, cantilevered ramp curves continuously as it rises 75 feet to the roof. A domed skylight covers the building and floods the interior with natural light. Works of art are displayed on the ground floor and in the 74 circular bays that line the walls of the ramp. A lower level auditorium accommodates 300 people.

In 1989, construction began on a major addition that will double available exhibition space. In 1990, the museum closed for restoration.

Hoffman Auto Showroom

Photo courtesy Mercedes-Benz North America

Mercedes-Benz Manhattan (currently)
430 Park Avenue New York, New York 10022
(212) 629.1666
No organized tours • Showroom hours are Monday through Friday,
9 a.m. to 5 p.m.; Saturday, 9 a.m. to 4 p.m.

1954

Wright used glass and steel, materials he called basic tools of machine-age architecture, to distinct advantage in his design of a Park Avenue showroom. The client, Maximilian Hoffman, was an early importer of European automobiles for the U.S. luxury car market. The curvilinear surfaces and mirrors visually expand this relatively limited ground-floor space at the same time they complement the sleek, gleaming contours of the vehicles.

Mercedes-Benz Manhattan has occupied the showroom since 1957. In 1981 they completed a restoration project that included installing a previously unexecuted, mirrored Mercedes-Benz insignia in the showroom ceiling, according to Wright's original design.

::

Francis Little House II
Living Room Reconstruction

Metropolitan Museum of Art, American Wing
Fifth Avenue at 82nd Street New York, New York 10028
(212) 879.5500 ext. 3791
Museum hours: Tuesday through Thursday and Sunday 9:30 a.m. to
5:15 p.m.; Friday and Saturday, 9:30 a.m. to 8:45 p.m. • Groups of 15
or more by appointment only • Contribution suggested, adults $6
• Handicapped accessible • Gift store

1912-1914

The living room of the Littles' Minnesota house was Wright's largest domestic
interior. Intended primarily as a public space for musical recitals and entertaining,
the room was designed as an independent pavilion. Access was gained through a
separate exterior entrance or from the main living area through a small door.

Every architectural and decorative detail contributes to the subtle and
sophisticated visual harmony of this vast space. Twelve paired art glass panels were
centered along each of the side walls. Originally the clear and opaque white glass
created a kind of decorative border framing views of Lake Minnetonka and the
surrounding woods. The art glass design continues in the clerestory windows and
five skylights that were lit from behind with electric lamps at night.

Narrow bands of white oak define the wall surfaces and extend across the
coved ceiling, which reaches a height of 14 1/2 feet.

The room's furnishings are original although Wright designed some of the
pieces for the Littles' first house in Peoria, Illinois. The Metropolitan Museum was
instrumental in saving significant parts of Wright's last great Midwestern Prairie
School residence before its demolition in 1972. The Little house library can be seen
in the Allentown Art Museum.

Meyers Medical Clinic

5441 Far Hills Avenue Dayton, Ohio 45429
(513) 435.0031
No regularly scheduled tours. Call to arrange a visit • Handicapped
accessible

1956

Of the nine buildings Wright designed in Ohio in the '50s, the Meyers Medical Clinic was the only commercial structure. The wide-angled plan includes a central entrance flanked by a "rotunda" to the south and a waiting/reception wing to the north. Here, floor-to-ceiling windows and doors afford patients an expansive view of the terrace and lawn beyond.

At the opposite end, wedge-shaped examination rooms with clerestory windows open onto a centralized work area for clinic staff. The interior and exterior walls are of brick. The original floor was red pigmented concrete.

The building continues in use as a medical clinic and has been renovated and restored by its present owner.

Price Tower

Photo courtesy Landmark Preservation Council Bartlesville, Oklahoma

39 OKLAHOMA

Northeast Sixth Street at Dewey Avenue Bartlesville, Oklahoma 74003
(918) 661.7471
Guided tours Thursdays at 1, 1:30 and 2 p.m. • Groups of 14 or more
by appointment only. Contact Landmark Preservation Council,
Box 941, Bartlesville, OK 74005 • Donation suggested • Limited
handicapped access

1952

When Harold C. Price approached Wright to design a building for his Bartlesville
pipeline construction firm, he envisioned a three-story, 15,000-square-foot structure.
Wright immediately rejected the concept as inefficient; and one year later he
presented Price with drawings for a 19-story, 37,000-square-foot, multi-use tower
that would serve as corporate headquarters for the company with additional space
for apartments and professional offices.

The structural precedent for this "tower in a country town" was an
unexecuted 1929 design for a New York City apartment building. Wright described
the building as a tree-like mast. Each concrete floor slab cantilevers out like the
branches of a tree from four interior vertical supports. Freed of their load-bearing
function, the exterior walls became ornamental screens. The angled faces of Price
Tower were constructed from sheets of stamped copper and gold-tinted glass.

The interior space of each floor was divided into four, diamond-shaped
modules. The 19th floor was reserved for Price's office and a rooftop garden
overlooking the city.

In 1981, Phillips Petroleum purchased the building. Three years later, the
American Institute of Architects recognized the tower with its prestigious "25 Year
Award" for enduring architectural design.

Francis Little House II
Library Reconstruction

Allentown Art Museum
Fifth & Court Street P.O. Box 117 Allentown, Pennsylvania 18105-0388
(215) 432.4333
Museum hours: Tuesday through Saturday, 10 a.m. to 5 p.m.; Sunday,
1 to 5 p.m. • Groups of 10 or more by appointment only • Donation
suggested • Handicapped accessible • Bookshop

1912-1914

The extraordinarily large and complex home Wright designed for Francis and Mary Little in Wayzata, Minnesota, was among the richest expressions of the Prairie School aesthetic. Before the building was demolished in 1972, critical sections were saved, including this library.

Originally located to the left of the home's asymmetrical entrance, the library functioned primarily as a reception area. Large art glass windows on the east and south walls overlooked a terrace and the lawn respectively. The west wall was lined with oak book shelves.

When the library was reconstructed, architects followed a scheme used elsewhere in the house and added the parallel bands of oak trim to the ceiling as well as concealed lighting. The furnishings are not original but are consistent with Wright's style of interior design. The barrel chairs are reproductions of those he designed for several homes.

The library is one of two intact spaces from the Littles' Minnesota property on exhibit. The Metropolitan Museum of Art in New York has reconstructed the living room in the museum's American Wing.

::

Beth Sholom Synagogue

Old York and Foxcroft Roads Elkins Park, Pennsylvania 19117
(215) 887.1342
Guided tours: Monday through Wednesday, 11 a.m. to 3 p.m.; Sunday,
9 a.m. to 1 p.m. (if no scheduled activities) • Groups by appointment
only • Free • Gift store

1954

The complex symbolism embodied in the design of this synagogue for a conservative congregation is the result of a close collaboration between Rabbi Mortimer J. Cohen and Wright. Every element of the structure's design was carefully calculated to reflect some aspect of Jewish faith, history or religious practice, and Americanism.

The building's hexagonal plan, according to Wright, mirrors the shape of cupped hands, as if the congregants were "resting in the very hands of God." Stairs leading from the entrance to the main sanctuary parallel the ascent of Mount Sinai. The pyramidal dome takes the form of the mountain, and the light penetrating its glass and plastic walls symbolizes the gift of the law.

Seating for 1100 people is arranged in triangular sections around the pulpit. A 40-foot concrete monolith, representing the two tablets given to Moses, forms a dramatic backdrop for the wooden ark containing one Torah for each of the 10 commandments. The aluminum and glass sculpture over the ark is entitled "Wings."

The building, completed in 1956, also contains a smaller, lower-level sanctuary, lounges, offices and meeting rooms.

::

Edgar J. Kaufmann House
Fallingwater

P.O. Box R Mill Run, Pennsylvania 15464
(412) 329.8501
Guided tours: April through mid-November, Tuesday through Sunday,
10 a.m. to 4 p.m. Mid-November through March, Saturday and
Sunday,11 a.m. to 4 p.m. In-depth tours and special weekend children's
tours by reservation only • In-depth tour $20; weekend tours $8; Tuesday
through Friday tours, adults $6, seniors $5, students $4 • No children
under 10. On-site childcare available. $2 per child per hour • No
photographs during tour • Bookshop and cafe

1936

The country home of Pittsburgh department store magnate Edgar J. Kaufmann
demonstrates Wright's mastery of nature and engineering in the service of art.
Fallingwater is the realization of Wright's romantic vision of man living in perfect
harmony with nature.

A waterfall fed by a mountain stream, dense forest and the rugged terrain
of southwestern Pennsylvania inspired the design of this extraordinary private
residence. Determined to build directly over the falls, Wright used reinforced
concrete and a cantilever system to extend the rock outcroppings of the site. The
natural rock and a masonry wall at the rear of the house anchor a series of terraces
or "concrete trays" that project out over the falls and seem to float above
the valley floor.

Rugged sandstone quarried on the site, concrete and glass form the exterior and interior fabric of the building. The first floor is essentially a single open space with stairs leading down to the stream. The upper floors are divided into bedroom suites, each opening onto a private terrace. Walls of glass open the interior to the surrounding tree tops. The Wright-designed furnishings are intact.

In 1939 Wright designed complementary guest quarters set into the hillside directly above the main house. In 1963 the Kaufmann family donated the property to the Western Pennsylvania Conservancy. The building is a National Historic Landmark.

Dallas Theater Center
Kalita Humphreys Theater

3636 Turtle Creek Boulevard Dallas, Texas 75219
(214) 526.8210
Guided tours by appointment only. Monday through Friday, 9 a.m. to
5 p.m. (when rehearsal not in progress) • Free • Handicapped
accessible

1955

Wright completed plans for two earlier theaters, but Dallas is the home of the only
commissioned theater ever executed from his designs. The reinforced concrete
structure is built into the hillside of a one-acre, wooded site in the center of the city.

Wright planned a zigzag approach from the parking lot to the entrance,
providing patrons with ample opportunity to view the irregular massing of the
building.

The modern theater, Wright said, should free the stage by eliminating the
traditional proscenium frame. His design includes a circular drum containing a 32-
foot revolving stage. The performing space can be extended through the use of the
fixed apron, side stages and balconies.

Other features of the building's design include dressing rooms on three
levels and ramps leading to production workshops beneath the auditorium. The
exposed lights, freight elevator and expanded foyer are later additions.

Pope-Leighey House

Woodlawn Plantation
P.O. Box 37 Mount Vernon, Virginia 22121
(703) 780.4000
March through December, daily tours from 9:30 a.m. to 4:30 p.m.;
January and February, Saturday and Sunday only, 9:30 a.m. to 4:30
p.m.• Adults $4; seniors and students through 12th grade $3; children
under five free • Limited handicapped access • No photographs
• Bookshop

1940

Wright designed this 1200-square-foot house for Washington journalist Loren Pope
and his wife at a total cost of $7000. Originally located in Falls Church, Virginia, the
building was moved to its present location after being donated to the National Trust
for Historic Preservation by its second owner Mrs. Robert Leighey.

Built of cypress, brick, and glass, the structure includes the flat roof,
recessed lighting, carport, heated floor slab and integral window design
characteristic of Wright's Usonian homes.

Seth Peterson Cottage

Mirror Lake State Park
Lake Delton, Wisconsin 53965
Guided tours the first Sunday in June and year-round the second
Sunday of each month, 2 to 5 p.m. Other times by appointment
only, call (608) 254.6051 or write: Seth Peterson Cottage
Conservancy, S1994 Pickerel Slough Road, Wisconsin Dells, WI
53965 • All ages $2 • Handicapped accessible

1958

This 900-square-foot building occupies a secluded promontory in one of Wisconsin's
most popular state parks. Originally the site was owned by young Seth Peterson
who asked Wright to design an intimate cottage to which he later planned to take
his bride.   Peterson's untimely death in 1960 left the house unfinished and
unoccupied.

The building was sold, completed and privately owned until 1966 when it
was purchased by the state. The small but functional cottage contains a combined
living and dining room, a kitchen, utility room, and bedroom. The stone incorporated in the building's design was hand-quarried at a local site. The exterior and
interior walls are sandstone; the fireplace, floor, and terrace are flagstone. The glass
west facade opens the interior to the surrounding trees and lake view.
Prolonged neglect and repeated vandalism reduced the cottage to near ruin. The
building is now undergoing rehabilitation.

Unitarian Meeting House

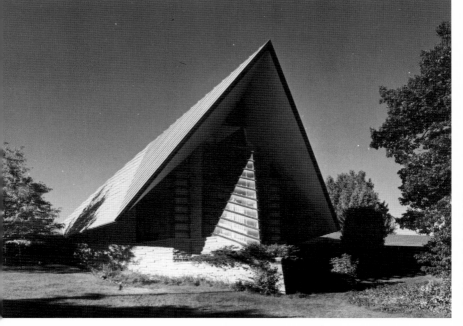

900 University Bay Drive Madison, Wisconsin 53705
(608) 233.9774
Guided tours: Mid-May through September, Tuesday through Friday,
1 to 4 p.m.; Saturday, 9 a.m. to noon. Other times by appointment
• Groups by appointment only • Minimum donation $2

1947

When Wright designed the Unitarian Meeting House, it was a hilltop "country church." The native limestone and oak building with its asymmetrical copper roof reflects Wright's belief that church design should be non-sectarian, "more earth-loving, with a deeper feeling for nature."

Commissioned in 1946, the church took five years to build. Members of the congregation hauled limestone to the site from a local quarry. Wright felt personally invested in the project as his parents were among the organization's earliest members. He accepted a minimal fee, offered the assistance of Taliesin apprentices and helped to raise funds by giving two lectures.

Wright's design is based on a diamond module. The form is evident in the floor pattern, the shape of the auditorium and hearth room when joined, as well as the stone pillars and planters. The auditorium with its soaring ceiling and glass prow can seat 340 people. A loggia leads to the west living room, where social functions are held.

The educational wing is a later addition.

::

S.C. Johnson and Son Administration Building

1936

Guest Relations Center
1525 Howe Street Racine, Wisconsin 53403
(414) 631.2154
Guided, half-hour tours by appointment only: Tuesday through Friday,
9:45 and 11:30 a.m., 1 and 2:45 p.m. • Children must be 14 or older
unless accompanied by an adult • Free • Tours do not include tower

Imagination, innovative technology and client confidence combined to produce a revolutionary design for the corporate headquarters of the S. C. Johnson Wax Company. Herbert F. Johnson, a successful executive and sympathetic manager, envisioned a building that would provide a functional, pleasant working environment at the same time it projected a modern corporate image for his growing family business. When completed in 1939, the building was hailed in the press as the greatest innovation since the skyscraper—a true glimpse of things to come.

Since "nature was not present" in the surrounding industrial landscape, the streamlined, curving brick face of the building is without conventional window openings. Instead, Wright "recreated nature" on the interior with a forest of slender tapering "dendriform" columns that extend 21 feet from floor to ceiling, where they widen to support the 20-foot wide concrete pads carrying the weight of the roof. The columns are constructed of high-strength concrete and steel mesh.

Wright allocated the interior space according to the flow of work through the corporate organization. The company's clerical workforce occupies the Great Workroom, middle managers the mezzanine, and executives the penthouse.

Wright's use of translucent glass tubing instead of transparent window glass was equally unprecedented. Forty-three miles of layered pyrex tubing form the horizontal bands beneath the mezzanine and below the cornice line, as well as the skylit openings around the column capitals. Natural light thus floods the interior space creating a workplace "as inspiring to live and work in as any cathedral ever was to worship in."

The building, which is a National Historic Landmark, also contains a theater, circular stairs and circular elevators. Wright designed the interior furnishings, including three-legged chairs and desks with swinging tills.

In 1944, Johnson returned to Wright to design new quarters for the company's research and development division. The resulting 14-story research tower is connected to the corporate offices by a covered bridge.

∷

Riverview Terrace Restaurant

The Spring Green (currently)
Highway 23 Spring Green, Wisconsin 53588
(608) 588.2571
No organized tours • Open daily May through November at 11 a.m.
Call for winter hours • Groups of 10 or more require reservations
• Handicapped accessible

1953

Situated on the left bank of the Wisconsin River, the Spring Green is the only restaurant designed by Wright. Steel trusses from the flight deck of the Ranger, a World War II aircraft carrier training ship, were used to support the 300-foot structure. Wright planned the original restaurant as a teahouse for Taliesin guests.

Construction began in 1957 but ended with the architect's death in 1959. When W.H. Keland acquired the plans and land, he commissioned the Taliesin Fellowship to complete the restaurant as part of a larger resort development. The restaurant officially opened in September 1967. Wright's wife Oglivanna is responsible for the interior design. The extension of the lounge in 1969 is the only departure from Wright's original design.

::

Taliesin

Highway 23 Spring Green, Wisconsin 53588
(608) 588.2511
Hillside Home School • Guided tours: May through October, daily,
9 a.m. to 4 p.m., hourly • Groups of 15 or more by appointment only
• Adults $6; children under 12 $3
Taliesin Walking Tour • Guided 1.5-hour tour of property. Departs
Hillside School. June through September, Monday through Saturday,
10:30 a.m. Call to confirm exact dates • $15 per person

1902-1925

Wright designed Hillside School, a progressive, coeducational boarding school for
his aunts Nell and Jane Lloyd Jones in 1902. The oak and ashlar-cut sandstone
building demonstrates his interest in using materials native to the site.

The original plan provided for a gymnasium, laboratory, drawing studio,
assembly hall and classrooms. In 1932, Wright remodeled the space to accommodate
the Taliesin Fellowship, an architectural training program. Changes included the
construction of a 5000-square-foot drafting room and the conversion of classrooms
and the gym to a gallery and theater.

In 1911, Wright designed Taliesin, his own residence and studio, nearby.
Despite devastating fires in 1914 and 1925, he continued to rebuild, each time
expanding the complex until it eventually comprised living quarters, work spaces,
offices, apartments, and numerous courtyards and terraces. On adjoining family
land, Wright designed Tan-y-deri, a house for his sister, as well as the buildings of
Midway Farm. An 1897 windmill, was also designed by Wright.

Until 1938, Taliesin was Wright's home; thereafter he spent winters at
Taliesin West in Scottsdale, Arizona, and returned each summer to Spring Green.
Taliesin is a National Historic Landmark.

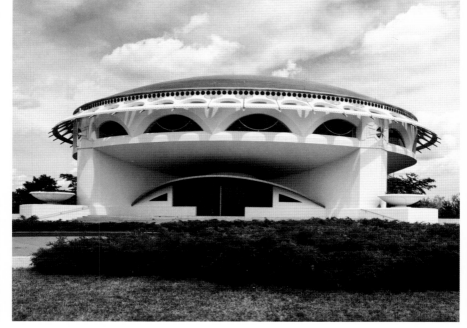

9400 West Congress Wauwatosa, Wisconsin 53225
(414) 461.9400
Guided tours by appointment only, Monday through Friday, 9 a.m. to
2:15 p.m.; 15 person minimum • All ages $1 • Appropriate attire
required • Bookshop

1956

Although Wright's design represents a distinct departure from traditional Byzantine church architecture, he retained the concept of a domed space and incorporated the symbols of the Greek Orthodox faith in his plan.

The design is based on a cross inscribed in a circle. Four equidistant, reinforced concrete piers support the structure and define the cross on the main floor. The lower level space accommodates 240 congregants. Circular staircases lead to additional seating for 560 above.

To completely encircle the structure, Wright planned a dome 106 feet in diameter with a maximum height of 45 feet. The concrete shell is not fixed but floats on thousands of steel bearings allowing for expansion and contraction. The original, blue tile exterior was replaced with vinyl membrane. The interior is gold, anodized aluminum.

Light enters the church through semicircular windows and a ring of 325 glass spheres crowning the upper wall.

::

Archives and Collections

ARIZONA
The Frank Lloyd Wright
Memorial Foundation
Taliesin West
Scottsdale, Arizona 85261
(602) 860.2700

CALIFORNIA
Getty Center for the History of Art
and Humanities
401 Wilshire Boulevard
Suite 400
Santa Monica, California 90401
(213) 458.9811

Smithsonian Archives of American Art
Henry Huntington Library
1151 Oxford Road
San Marino, California 91108
(818) 405.7847

DISTRICT OF COLUMBIA
Manuscript Division
Library of Congress
Thomas Jefferson Building, Room 3004-5
Washington, D.C. 20540
(202) 707.5387

Prints and Photographs Division
Historical American Buildings Survey
Library of Congress
James Madison Building, Room 337
Washington, D.C. 20540
(202) 707.6399

ILLINOIS
Burnham Library
Art Institute of Chicago
Michigan Avenue at Adams Street
Chicago, Illinois 60603
(312) 443.3666

Oak Park Public Library
834 Lake Street
Oak Park, Illinois 60302
(708) 383.8200

Research Center
Frank Lloyd Wright Home and Studio
Foundation
951 Chicago Avenue
Oak Park, Illinois 60302
(708) 848.1976

NEW YORK
Buffalo and Erie County Historical Society
25 Nottingham Court
Buffalo, New York 14216
(716) 873.9644

University Archives
State University of New York at Buffalo
420 Capen Hall
Buffalo, New York 14260
(716) 636.2916

Architecture and Design Study Center
Museum of Modern Art
11 West 53rd Street
New York, New York 10019
(212) 708.9547

Avery Architectural and Fine Arts Library
Columbia University
534 W. 114th Street
New York, New York 10027
(212) 854.3068

Department of American Decorative Art
Metropolitan Museum of Art
Fifth Avenue at 82nd Street
New York, New York 10028
(212) 535.7710

WISCONSIN
State Historical Society of Wisconsin
816 State Street
Madison, Wisconsin 53703
(608) 262.3338

Exhibits

Prairie Archives
Milwaukee Art Museum
750 N. Lincoln Memorial Drive
Milwaukee, Wisconsin 53202
(414) 271.9508

WYOMING
American Heritage Center
University of Wyoming
Box 3924
University Station
Laramie, Wyoming 82071
(307) 766.6385

ILLINOIS
David and Alfred Smart Gallery
Cochrane-Woods Art Center
University of Chicago
5550 S. Greenwood Avenue
Chicago, Illinois 60637
(312) 702.0200

Department of Architecture
Art Institute of Chicago
Michigan Avenue at Adams Street
Chicago, Illinois 60603
(312) 443.3949

MICHIGAN
Domino's Center for Architecture & Design
44 Frank Lloyd Wright Drive
Ann Arbor, Michigan 48106
(313) 930.3818

MINNESOTA
Department of Decorative Arts
Minneapolis Institute of Arts
2400 Third Avenue South
Minneapolis, Minnesota 55404
(612) 870.3101

KANSAS
Edwin A. Ulrich Museum of Art
Wichita State University
Wichita, Kansas 67208
(316) 689.3664

Index